Coffee on the pavement

Poems by Pam Pointer

$\mathcal{F}$ir$\mathcal{S}$t erve Publishing

First Serve Publishing
9 Bishops Drive, East Harnham, Salisbury SP2 8NZ

Coffee on the Pavement
Copyright © Pam Pointer 2012
Design: Nicky Edwards

www.pampointer.co.uk
pampointer26@yahoo.co.uk

ISBN 978-178035-460-6

First published 2012 by
FIRST SERVE PUBLISHING
An imprint of Upfront Publishing of Peterborough, England.

Contents

The antidote to football

"Pound the pitch with purpose!"
demand frustrated fans.
"Goals are what would please us,
not slip-shod feet and hands."

Groans and moans and boos, too,
"Our lads must get a grip!
No loss or draws, we beg you;
Don't let more matches slip."

Football's not essential,
Try cricket's gentle charm.
Tennis, rugby, netball,
Those games should keep you calm.

Run an egg and spoon race,
Play ping-pong to and fro,
Swim some lengths, lift some weights,
See your muscles grow.

Football; let's forget it!
Alternatives exist,
Ones that hardly ever get
your knickers in a twist.

Autumn hedgerow

Mildewing blackberries fester
behind spiders' fairy fences
of strong, silken webs
whose owner occupiers
patiently reconstruct
rudely ruined traps
set for unsuspecting prey,
and destroyed by purple-stained fingers.

Battle for the skies

Crabby crow
in parsoned black
caws crossly,
flaps, frets and fights,
defending unfenced airspace,
while wide-winged and watchful,
his targeted buzzard,
in sun-kissed regal raiment
floats fearlessly,
unfazed, unhurried.
No crow commotion quells
fortune's felicity.

Boscombe Pier

Sleek lines stretch from shore to sea
In stunning simplicity
Understated Boscombe Pier

Strong lines hang from rail to sea
In quiet anticipation
Fishing reels of Boscombe Pier

Sun-kissed human flesh turns red
In burning embarrassment
Either side of Boscombe Pier

Surf banks hide beneath the sea
In quiet and sorry silence
Deep and east of Boscombe Pier

Shushing waves of rippling sea
Sparkling serendipity
Lap the sands by Boscombe Pier.

Buddleias

Buddleias bloom
boldly
brashly
beautifully
mutinously
multitudinously
taking their humble place
in litter strewn wasteland
by railway lines.

Bird on a wire

Alone but not lonely
Still as stone but not petrified
Grave as death but fully alive.

Bird on a wire,
wrapped in dawn's bright sunlight,
gazes silently at drowsy hills,
and green unripened wheat
below unending blue, where
silver trails hint at man's relentless rush,
echoed below in the distant drone
of invisible traffic moving through corridors
of heavily-dressed summer trees.

Solitary souls drive on,
driven by need or greed,
to bleak boxes
where Windows whirrs in blind-drawn rooms,
where workers wage war on procedures
and speak soundlessly on line.

He, oblivious to shocks through power-crazed pylons,
sits on the loop of his private public line
that spans space, that takes modernity
to those who take it for granted,
and couldn't live without it.

Of this he's unaware.

He hears the chattering classes
of buntings, warblers, larks,
hidden below amongst sturdy stalks and upright ears,
And sits,
silently,
in harmony with nature
at quiet companionship with his unseen Maker
undaunted
untainted
unharmed,
still;
and instils a calm tranquillity
in those who pause to watch and ponder,
who use this brief moment
where cares are absent
and who, if wise,
carry the bird on a wire
into the day ahead.

The buzzard

Silently
he hovers,
dips,
swoops,
and rises to
glide in
joyous abandon;
then breaks his silence
with a single mew,
that makes me glance up
from muddied earth-bound gaze
to soar,
momentarily,
with him.

Can I wear socks with sandals?

Can I wear socks with sandals
Or would it be a scandal?
Those of fashion
Have a passion:
They deem it shameful,
(I find it painful)
But if bare feet are cursed
Socked feet are worse.
Look down nose
At my poor toes
Bent bunioned feet
Are not a treat.

Can I wear socks with sandals?
It's surely NOT a scandal.
But if folk can't cope
Well, let them mope,
Ignore me, scorn me, shun me.
I can, I could, I should, I WILL.

Lurid lime or shocking pink
Such bright socks will make them blink...
Or, lime on left and pink on right,
What a statement! What a sight!
Anything for joy and ease
(even if it fails to please.)
Can I wear socks with sandals?
Why not! I LIKE a scandal.

The champions

Rafa's not a faffer
out there on Centre Court,
And Roger's not a dodger;
you saw how hard he fought,
But even kings can falter,
so the pecking order alters:
There's Laver, Newcombe, Emerson,
McEnroe and Ashe,
All wore the crown with true renown
for skill and great panache.
And Sampras, Hewitt, Agassi,
Edberg, Becker, Cash,
Thrilled and chilled spectators with
their serve and lob and smash.
But no man reigns forever,
however good he is,
Injuries and passing years
mean slower legs, less dash.
Eventually they bow out;
let's face it, they decline,
And the tennis role of kingship
is passed on down the line...

Before we leave the champions,
let's ponder for a mo
The roll-call of the also-rans
whose ball skills wowed us so:
Rosewall, Stolle, Lendl, Roche,
they fought, alas, for naught,
They never won at Wimbledon,
Despite prowess on court.
So here's the burning question,
the one that's always asked,
Just who's the best that ever played,
Oh, what a tricky task.
Who's the one in favour?
I've given you this guide
Is it Federer or Laver?
Please, can *you* decide?

Coffee on the pavement

Sitting on the pavement has become an English fashion,
In market towns and cities we do it with a passion,
Find an empty table and a hard and wobbly chair,
Then plonk your bottom on it, take time to stop and stare.

Breakfast for the workers then coffee for the shirkers,
Later, ladies lunching then, after school, more munching
By 6th form boys, apple-pied, watching girls, all doe-eyed,
What is this café culture that has us in such rapture?

Should I study history to solve the café mystery?
In London, many moons ago, the coffee house was strong, so
Did Paris copy us? Hey, be careful, or they'll fuss,
Don't create a Channel storm, France's cafés are the norm.

Coffee on the menu is a complicated business,
Requiring skills at language and a quick go at analysis:
Latte, mocha, decaff, cappuccino or espresso,
Americano, no cream, or a hefty mochaccino.

(All that fussy foam, I'd be better off at home,
With instant in a mug and without the smokers' fug.)

Conkers

Conkers burst from down-lined homes
to lie waiting
for eager little hands.
Alas, their shine when
disconnected from the source of life
soon ceases
and shrivelled specimens are thrown
to lie in wait through winter's weary weeks,
buried beneath leaves
trodden under mud
until a day when they
burst
and shoot
and Spring is proud to start again.

Covent Garden in June

Noisy, bright and colourful,
exuding fun and laughter,
Covent Garden beckons
with music, arts and crafts, yes,
tourists, young and old alike,
as part of London roving
sample all on offer
in frenzied treasure-troving.
Have their portraits painted by an
artist wielding paint brush, then
head for café table
before the lunchtime rush, when
men and girls from offices
turn up to join the battle,
sipping milky lattes,
exchanging tittle-tattle.
Shunning such commotion
we choose elsewhere to chatter;
lowly, hard and grubby
it may be but, no matter;
Like Eliza Dolittle
we sit there in the gutter
eating baked potatoes
with cheese and oozing butter;
thinking how it used to be
before a tourist target,
when flowers and fruit and
vegetables made Covent Garden market.

Creation

Did
God make
trunk call for
mammoth task of
shaping elephant?

Did
God make
bee-line for
honey-pot when
buzzed on day of rest?

Did
God ask,
"Which comes first,
chicken or egg,
in pecking order?"

Did
God wear
kid gloves to
form nanny goat,
or ramshackle ones?

The CV of a one year old

I am only one
But I am one.

I can walk
- after a fashion;
My reversing skills are a bit suspect
and I sometimes miss
when I try to sit down.

I'm a good climber
onto the sofa or
up the stairs,
but not so good at
coming down
down
down
down.
Bump.

I like to explore
leaves
and mud in plant pots
and spread dusty compost
on the carpet
and swish it with my fingers.
I look round to see if anyone's watching,
smile if they are and
refrain from doing what I shouldn't,
But if nobody's there, I have a ball.

I can also
roll a ball and
knock beaker towers down
and wreck my sister's jigsaw
and cuddle my doll
and take Teddy for walks in his buggy.

I am only one
but I am one.

December visitors

JACK FROST
He comes;
nips nose,
fingers, toes;
patterns panes
with feathered veins.

WINTER SUN
A reluctant riser,
he hangs silently
in the wintry sky;
His brief waking hours
bring cheer, and
spirits soar to view
the golden orb that
plunges, in a blaze of glory,
back to bed.

JESUS CHRIST
He comes
from glorious light
to hidden womb,
through birth canal
to a dark world
where light
heralds his arrival
and a few
ordinary people
hear good news
and see
the vulnerable
venerable
Saviour.

The fags and the fag-nots

Crave fag
Puff smoke
Sip Coke
Eye bloke
Life's no joke:
Poked outside
Rain-soaked .

Smug folk
Look down
Stare, frown,
Down town
How they scowl:
Woe betide.
Tar-choked.

Down, out
Unclean
Unseen
Routine
Nicotine
Must decide.
No joke.

Foggy night

Fog descends
slowly at first
with still a hint of pale stars,

then, with swift stealth
and in smothering silence,
closes in cruel embrace.

Birds have long since
given up daytime chatter
and evening praise;

twigs hold pearl tears
in uneasy tension,
as yet unreleased.

In the isolating silence
a woman walks alone
with dampened hair and spirit

On, on, in automatic mode,
with steady rhythmic beat,
not knowing where she goes.

Yet even within her shrouded soul,
bruised body, and numbed mind,
there is a thought

that she isn't quite alone,
that beyond, behind, above the fog
somewhere, steady stars still shine.

God

God...
Comes where heaven meets earth, living in both as Emmanuel.
Close beside me, in front of me, behind me, above me, within me.
Cares for me more than anybody on earth ever could or would
    want to.
Carries me when I'm too weary to walk or too troubled to talk.
Caresses me when I'm sad, hugs me tight and lets my tears splash
    on him.
Calms me as I walk in his hills and in woods, as I listen to him in
    birdsong.
Challenges me to keep him as my focus when I'm so easily
    distracted.
Cheers me all the way through life's marathon, and then helps me
    over the line.

God spoke to me this morning

God spoke to me this morning
in an unexpected way;
no furious wind to split the hills
or shatter ancient rocks,
no chasms from an earthquake,
no bush fire's awful shock,
and no soft whispered gentle words
to start the daytime clock.

God spoke to me this morning
in an awe-inspiring way;
I took a path less travelled by
through woods in early spring,
my steps and voice were silent
and I saw sweet nature bring
a wealth of unimpeded joy
in this, its morning fling.

God spoke to me this morning
in a cheerful, direct way:
a robin, perched up in a tree
against the dawning sky,
olive-backed with orange chest,
looked down with beady eye.
his tuneful trilling thrilled my soul,
God's message: "I'm close by!"

Hastings Pier

Black-burnt buildings
and fast-rusting railings
deny defeat,
defy death.
This once-proud pier
with still-strong struts
waits,
wave-washed,
for rebirth.

High risers

High rise city slickers
In sparkling glass-clad towers,
Tread marble floors, and bicker
On money, greed and power.

High-rise city dwellers
In concrete Sixties' towers,
Climb urine-stinking stairwells
Where poverty devours.

High-rise city fixers
Exist in both those towers,
Cocaine and fags, those tricksters
Turn poor and wealthy sour.

One group thinks they've made it:
Glamour, riches, fame
Champagne a prerequisite
When moved to entertain,
Yet beneath the celebration
An emptiness invades,
Banishing elation
A loneliness pervades,
Caviar and sharp suits
From Fortnums, Savile Row,
Superficial attributes
Consumed and stained, mere show.

The other group can't stand it:
Clamour, hitches, shame,
Claim their meagre benefits
And queue to sign their name,
Angst and deprivation
Much cause to be afraid,
Joy-denying deflation
A dreary barricade,
Burger bar and jog suits
From cheap shops down the road,
Beneficial attributes?
Consumed, and stained, no go.

His turn to get the dinner

Got a job at the hob
It's down to me to make the tea
Got a date with a plate
Just done the toast (but mustn't boast)
Got the beans, found the means
to open tin and tip them in
Got the pan, steady, man!
It's heating up, soon time to sup
Got the meal, no big deal
It's ready now; a taste... Oh wow!
Got to say, mere child's play
"It's time to dine, oh wife of mine!"

I'm on the train to Waterloo

I'm on the train to Waterloo to meet
a man called Walter Drew who wants to go
to Timbuktu with Fanciful his cockatoo,
a silly bird who squawks so much
I'd like to kick him into touch but if
they get to Timbuktu I won't see either
quite so much. I've told him how to travel
there, the longest route by train, not air.
I'll ship them off without a care and hope
they stay at least a year.

In Bodmin Jail

In Bodmin jail
Do not pass Go
In chains
Do not pass Go
In jail
Weeping
In stocks
Incapable
Inconsolable
Interminable
In jail
Do not pass Go

In praise of Marmite

Cheers for Marmite whose
yellow sunshine head
entices me to delve deep
into dark depths
to catch the pungency
then savour the flavour
I feed my brain
with its vitamins
Bs are beneficial so
this B-stuffed goo
fits the bill perfectly
if you pretend it's free from salt.

Lying in bed on a snowy morning

Curled under covers thick and deep,
But much too cold to stay asleep,
I slowly open heavy eye
As gritting lorry rumbles by.

Through pale curtains orange light
Must wink its message through the night:
Beware the silent flakes of snow
Take care, it's freezing hard, you know.

Though very dark it's clear to tell
That morning comes – I know it well:
Mute clink of bottles, whirring float,
Spells frozen milk with frosted coat.

Now across the dawning stillness,
Largely undeterred by chillness,
Comes the thin clear morning chorus,
Joyful songsters up to cheer us.

Crunching crisply, heavy footfall,
Treading hard-packed icy snowfall,
Our whistling postman comes with torch
To leave some letters in the porch.

Early risers call a greeting
To each other, brief and fleeting,
Car engine starts and coughs and splutters
As snow across the window flutters.

Now the rudest sound of morning:
Bedside clock shrieks notes of warning,
No longer can I stay in bed
And rest my still so sleepy head.

So, off with bed-socks, on with shoes,
Warm porridge turns away the blues,
For I have promises to keep,
And jobs to do before I sleep,
And jobs to do before I sleep.

Man's glory - temporarily scuppered by an inconsiderate volcanic ash cloud

O man, O man!
Your greatness is seen in all the world,
Your praise reaches up to the skies;
It is sung by TV and Google;
You are safe and secure from all your enemies,
You stop everyone who opposes you.

When I look at the sky which you have filled,
At the planes and vapour trails which you set in place
What is God? You don't think of him!
Mere God? You don't care for him.

Man, you are superior to everything else!
You crown yourself with glory and honour,
You appoint yourself over everything you make,
You place yourself over all creation:
Sheep and cattle, and the wild animals too;
The birds and the fish,
Sea creatures, vulnerable people...
And especially over *your* creations.

O man, O man!
Your greatness is seen in all the world
Until a volcano bursts
From restless depths not yet conquered,
To spew through glacial ice
A moving molten mountain
That rises in magnificent majesty
Declaring its greater strength,

Its deeper, loftier power
That confuses, confounds and renders impotent
Man's misapprehension of himself and his creations.

O God! *Our* God?
You whom man's ignored, rejected, thrown out
As an irrelevant non-entity in his modern world.
Do you scorn, deride, ignore, discard him?
Leave him to muddle through his self-made murky ash cloud?
No. For you tell man that
You made him inferior only to yourself,
You crowned him with glory and honour
And came to rescue him from his self-absorption,
Self-congratulation, and ill-fated self-sufficiency.

Speak in the stunned silence of the skies
Whisper through fresh spring leaves
Quieten ever shrill voices of misguided man who
Still thinks he's in charge,
Beckon him to join you as he turns to wait in line
To hear his name called for the onward journey
Into life.

*Read Psalm 8 for God's view of the value of the created world and
of human beings.*

March dance

Leggy lambs
leap
for joy,
gambol in an
innocent dance
that belies
the gamble of
all-too-brief
lives

Dancing daffs
drift
in lawns,
swagger and toss
elegant heads
to trumpet
the coming of
another
Spring

Tangled twigs
spurt
star-gold
forsythia
in bursts of mirth
that brighten
winter-weary
hearts and tired
minds

Blackthorn's blooms
bud
blossom
round spiky thorns
snowy clusters
herald the
cherry blossoms
that soon will
bloom

Midsummer night

The golden gleam of sunset
Has scarce slipped out of sight
Before the glow of sunrise
Defies the hours of night.

A hasty moon comes swiftly
And glows, ice-cool and calm,
Its paling face fades quickly
At birds' wake-up alarm.

No agony at bedtime
The darkness brings no fear
Tranquillity, a glad time,
This short night of the year.

Jail bird

He gulps a rush of hot London air,
blows out, in relief-rich celebration,
long sigh of fetid breath
from long days and nights
inside.

Inside out,
outside in,
in, out, in, out,
shake it all about
in temporary delirium tremens.

Where to go? What to do?
Who to see?
He knows a mate
who'll fix him up:
a crack at this,
a snort of that,
a tot of this,
a pint of that.
Out, in, out, in,
breathe,
absorb,
live.
Out,
In,
Back in.
Repeat from beginning.

Moonlight flit

The moon glides
slowly, steadily,
across the open-curtained window,
and stares
from its full face
onto the figure of a
wakeful woman
who lies still
and stares back,
seeing its cool, calm light,
and myriad sparkling diamonds
that dance on the
rippling sea that breaks
on the shore below.
She rises quietly,
slides out of bed,
dresses,
steals to the door
and slips out,
leaving her sleeping partner
unaware
of the beckoning light
that takes her.
By dawn she is gone.

No one else feeds pigeons

Scruffy, scrapping scavengers
Under the arch, every day;
Squalid, soiling, unsavoury,
Under our feet, in the way;
Snacks of seedy bits scatter
Under her hand, go astray,
Spilling, fouling, littering;
Undeniable disarray.

> No one else feeds pigeons,
> But she does.

Undermined, unloved, unkempt,
Under coat, quite threadbare, frayed,
Undesirable, undone,
Underwear, grubby and grey;
Underclass of underpass,
Shuffling, shifty, shadowy
Subject of undisguised contempt;
Shift! Shoo! Undeterred, she stays.

> No one else feeds pigeons
> But she does.

Pesky, preying, parasite,
Scuffling scrounger's downward-gaze,
Picking, pecking pilferer,
Pitiful, unpleasant ways;
Pitiful... painful... pathos.
There but for the God of grace
Go I, and the rest of us
Who live an easier way,
But, embarrassed by ourselves,
Pray that she'll go away.

No one else feeds pigeons
But she does.

Ponderous pigeons, puzzled, come
In dribs and drabs this Saturday,
Wait in vain for scraps to surface
On the shady flag-stoned pathway;
Ignored by market-stallholders,
Shoppers, and those on holiday,
Pretty tourist town, resplendent,
Doesn't notice she's gone away.

No one else feeds pigeons...

Now and forever

Blushing blossom against a blue sky,
bright fresh leaves on birch and beech,
bold brassy dandelion,
shy delicate primrose,
and an ever-present chorus of praise
from robin, thrush and blackbird,
combine to celebrate Spring's burgeoning
on this English April evening.
God's in his heaven
and on earth all's well with the world.

All's well with the world?
It may be, here, on the surface,
but somewhere near or far
the brightness hides an underlying darkness
where fear, despair and sorrow
tremble,
plunge,
and weep.
Where, because of one despicable act,
lives are marred and scarred,
bodies hurt, hearts ache
and outraged cries rise to the God of heaven
who came to earth.

Came to earth to meet those
anguished howls and silent screams,
down, down to earth, to be humiliated,
to be bruised and battered, mocked and tortured,
to die in the ultimate empathetic act of love;
to share with us in our trials;
to bring life out of the destructive forces that
wreak decay and death on body, mind and spirit;
to show the sweeping canvas of
redemption, resurrection and renewal.

Be still.
Listen.
The robin still sings,
a glimpse of God for us to hear and see,
light in darkness, joy in grief.
He who sees the sparrow fall,
who makes the robin sing
and the blossom bloom,
sees you,
now,
just as you are,
weeps with you, holds you,
and points you to the day of promise
when there will be no more death,
no more grief or crying or pain,
just the beauty of healing leaves
and the sparkling water of life.
Paradise perfection.
In the presence of the Life-Giver.
For you.
Forever.

Over-indulgence

Is it just a quirk of fate,
My tendency to put on weight?
Nothing seems to make me light
Unless I banish food from sight.
Yesterday I sat and ate
Buttered crumpets, licked the plate,
Then had chocolate – just a bite...
And wondered why my skirt felt tight.

Pacifying the lawn man

What's wrong with moss?
Who gives a toss
if it's in the grass
as bold as brass?

You grab a rake,
get sore and ache,
then you try to weed,
put down a feed.

Short-lived repair,
and you despair
for the moss comes back,
alas, alack!

Think Donna Moss,
Kate, Stirling Moss,
to distract your brain
from hurt and pain.

There, sit you down,
wipe off that frown,
and enjoy her face,
their grace, his race.

Gone, furrowed brow!
You're rested now;
so let's face the facts
and make a pact:

Don't fret and scream
or make a scene;
in the game of lawn
you're just a pawn.

It's soft, it's green,
so be serene,
and agree to say,
"Moss stays, OK?"

Phoney

She sits on floor,
Legs angled,
Soles of feet together.
Perfectly balanced.
Concentrating...

Then from a handset held to ear
Come words that make her
Smile and nod and
Check an invisible diary
That lies between her knees.

Pretend pencil poised,
Another nod then
Vital scribbles
Trace paisley squiggles.
"Thank you... see you... bye."
Handset clicks onto cradle at her side.

Long look at diary.
Numbers dialled.
Bell tinkles.
Phone to ear.
"Oh hello Emma, how are you?"
Giggle, giggle.
"Can you come for tea today?"
Deep sigh.
"Tomorrow?
Pause.
"Good."

Job done.
Phone's pushed away,
Its eyes bobbing up and down
And wheels spin
Till it crashes
Into Teddy by the toy cupboard.

Then hands to floor,
Bottom raised,
She pushes herself to her feet and
Toddles off to discover
New ways to mimic Mum.

Ode to mouses

Mice, should that be mouses?
Sit smugly on my desk
Feeling safe as houses
Thinking they know best

One is on the laptop
A flat black slender thing
Looks all calm and friendly
But likes to have a fling

Genteel looks belie her
She's vicious when she's crossed
Best to just ignore her,
Think she's sick, or worse.

The other little mouse
is tailed and grey and fat
Thinks she's far superior
Sitting on her mat

Hold her at her sides
They glow bright red with pride
Puffed up little madam
Sat there by my side

Needed for a purpose
To help me write this tale
Mouses, you can stay here
Else my work will fail

Pig

There's something rather infra dig
About the carcass of a pig
Being carried by a man whose white
But blood-stained coat is quite a sight.
On shoulder high, in belly flop,
The luckless pig enters the shop.

He may lack life but still looks real,
Not yet the basis of a meal,
But once inside the opened door
His fate is closed forever, for
Butcher, busy as a beaver,
Gets to work with shining cleaver.

But when it comes to roasted pork
With apple sauce, how we all talk
Of tender meat so full of flavour,
Something that our taste buds savour,
And as for sausages and mash,
We're always ready with our cash.

The moral of this gruesome tale
Is not to boost the butcher's sale
Nor yet promote a veggie's voice,
But call us all to make our choice
With wisdom, clarity and wit -
You can't have your pig and eat it.

Relax

I'm tense today,
"Relax!" they say.
But tension grips
With vicious clips.
I'm so hard-pressed
With constant stress,
Muscles tight,
Knuckles white,
Head bent down,
Pout and frown.
"Relax!" they say,
Relax? No way!
Twiddle thumbs,
Fingers drum.

Rest awhile,
Shut that file,
Close the door,
Relax the jaw,
Stretch the hands
Like rubber bands,
Smooth the face,
Slow your pace.
Try a smile
For a while.
Still your mind,
Just unwind.
Blot out fear,
Peace is near.

Shut your eyes,
See blue skies,
Tranquil seas,
Gentle breeze.
Pleasant things
Peace, joy brings.
Calm your will.
Then be still.

Be still.
Stay still.
Still.
Yes, still.
Listen in silence
To the silent whisper
Of God.
And be at peace.

Robbie

Worn clothing,
worn carelessly,
Coating for careworn body.
Listless eyes
lift to plead in languorous tones
and piteous whisper:
'Spare some change!'
Change for
change of clothes,
for food or fags,
drink or drugs?
Anything to relieve
for a blissful moment
the awfulness of
sitting hunched on bum-numbing pavement
watching legs go by.
Border collie,
head on paws,
ears flat,
gives warmth to
the arm that holds him.
Is he hungry too
for food and drink,
for freedom to run with long bounding strides,
his sleek, glossy coat stretched
in the joy of
leaping and frollicking through green meadows,
tongue hanging in doggy smile?
And does his master, too,
long for freedom to stretch up tall,

head held high
to meet the eyes of those who
pass him by?
Free to shed the slumping burden of homelessness,
the relentless treadmill of theft and fix
that leave him
blanketed in threadbare bleakness,
silent and alone.

Seve Links
(remembering golfer Seve Ballesteros who died 2011)

Marram grass
sways sensually
through windswept dunes
but fails to seduce

Seve stares silently
at the true target
yards distant

His gaze shifts
Head bows to dimpled ball
For second shot

Intense concentration

Hands grip club
Short back-swing
Connect
Follow-through
Wait...
Flings head back
Not close enough
Edge of green
Light rough

Marram murmurs

Undeterred
Undistracted
Head bends again
Caution
Hit
Pause...
Yes!
Head up
Fist pumps
Broad grin
Successful sink

And the marram grass waits
for a lesser man

Poppies

Lying low, in
scratchy stubble
and feathered grasses,
scarlet-clad poppies
bloom
bold and bright

Along the field margins,
receding into the distance,
their uniformed line stretches
across the hills
into infinity

But come closer, for
hundreds of dewy meshes,
sparkling silver,
entwine poppies, grass and straw
in strong, strangling embrace

Thus entrapped,
bowed, bent, beleaguered,
their freedom held at bay,
they wait,
unhurried,
for release
or death.

The car's got hiccups

The car's got hiccups
and arrhythmia and
stutters and splutters
and generally protests
at being used,
abused, misused,
when all it wants to do is
retire.

Cranky, it is, and
too sensitive for its own good,
which is more or less
what the garage man said.
"Crank sensor,
the computer told us."

But it's fixed now,
so no more excuses,
no more protests.
Just run smoothly,
steadily, reliably,
and forget
retirement.

The cow's in the meadow

Daisy,
Chewing cud,
Stands and stares,
Knee-deep in buttercups.

Too baffling for words

School taught me a lot of facts
to help me in my life,
but fax machines defeat me still
and e-mails cause me strife.

Then, the cat sat on the mat,
proud queen of street and house;
today the mat is on the desk
and perched on top, a mouse.

I went fishing as a lad
with hook and line and net;
today I sit in front of screen
and surf but don't get wet.

Mother took me to the doc
when I had flu or spots;
the docs I see most often now
are ones that follow dots.

Cuddling babies as a dad
they snuggled up on lap;
but lap-tops now provide much more
for business girls or chaps.

Mobiles slowly spun around,
quite silent and discreet,
but shrill tones now disturb the peace
on trains, in shops and streets.

Years ago, when twenty-two
I walked to work with Jim;
the gym is reached by car today,
a treadmill keeps him slim.

Partners helped me in the firm,
confusion reigns today,
a wife, a husband, lover, friend
all partners - straight or gay.

Sue, my wife of forty years
is gay and nicely fat,
but sue is what they'll do to folk
who misuse words like that.

Vital words, banal, oblique,
we speak and squeak and shriek...
I'll persevere, though past my peak,
with brave new world's bleak speak.

The passing of Woolworths

Popping into Woolworths was the natural thing to do
When you wanted pots of paint, or balls of string or glue,
Ladybird pyjamas, pairs of socks, umbrellas too,
Things you couldn't get in Woolworths were, quite frankly, few.
Roses for the garden and brushes for the loo,
Plastic bins, forsythia, oh nothing was taboo.
Tulip bulbs and light bulbs, or a cuddly kangaroo,
Skipping ropes and teddy bears, toy boats complete with crew,
Games galore at Christmas time – and decorations too,
Books of bedtime stories about fairies, trains or Pooh,
"How to" books of recipes for curry, jam, ragout,
How to put up shelves, or what to look for at the zoo.
Woolworths on a Saturday was where to rendevous,
"Meet me at the pick'n'mix between half one and two!"
Fill a bag with Smarties, yellow, orange, red and blue,
Toffees, humbugs, chocolates in bright wrappers to unscrew.
Spend an hour or even more in Woolworths, time just flew
Such times we will remember for we loved it through and through.
Now it's gone for good, a fact we'll never cease to rue
For popping into Woolworths was the natural thing to do.

Were they there?

Were angels really there that night,
Shining from on high?
Did they join the stars to light
The black-domed night-time sky?

Were shepherds really there that night,
Tending lambs and sheep?
Did they rush, alert and bright,
To see a babe asleep?

Were oxen really there that night,
And donkeys, chewing straw?
Did they watch the tender sight
From by the stable door?

Were they really there that night,
The pair from Nazareth?
Did they truly think it right –
A manger for his birth?

Were they really there that night,
Or is it just a dream?
Did old masters take delight
In making up such scenes?

Was God really there that night,
Directing from on high?
Or was he simply wrapped up tight,
Alive, but born to die?

Help me in my puzzled plight
To know if it is true,
Fly me now to heaven's height
To see a new world-view.

White Christmas

We dreamed of a white Christmas
Then wished it hadn't come
As leaden skies descended
And snow made fingers numb.

At first it looked a picture,
Pure white 'neath bright blue sky,
With gleeful children tossing
Their snowballs long and high.

But soon the snow compacted
And bumps and falls prevailed
As wheels spun and feet slipped
And promised journeys failed.

Oh, dream instead of sunshine
Of cricket Ashes won,
Of warmer days with family
Of beach and sun and fun.

Winter gale

With a song of sighs and sobs
skeletal trees sway to the rhythm of the wind
which, fitful and capricious,
flings brittle arms and twisted twiglet fingers
down to muddied earth.
Strewn haphazardly,
by Nature's infanticidal acts,
they lie, severed from life,
waiting for burial or burning,
while high above,
their stricken sisters, with soughing songs of sorrow
dance on, to the music of the wind.

Yeah -yeah

Did the Beatles start it
with she loves you yeah yeah yeah
or have we always done it:
this replacing yes with yeah?

Why do modern speakers
always answer with yeah-yeah?
Oh don't they know it freaks us
hearing double-barrelled yeahs?

Language is evolving,
yep, it never stays the same
so, priest-like, we're absolving
those we'd really like to blame.

Rules are there for breaking,
Oh, it's easy when you try,
and, yeah, (not yes,) I'm making
sure this poem goes awry:

So, let your yes be yes
and your no be no,
your yea be yea
and your nay be nay,
your yeah be yeah
and your neah be neah,
your yar be yar
and your nar be nar,
your yep be yep
and your nope be nope,

Your yeah be…
yeah right
and your no be…
no way!

Yeah, yeah, yeah
Yeah-yeah
Yeah
Wha'ever
Aw'right?
Right
Cool
Sorted.